THE GUIDE TO *Basket Weaving*

CREATIVE WEAVING WITH COCONUT PALMS

ISLAND HERITAGE
Honolulu, Hawai'i

DEDICATION

This book is dedicated to the Hawaiian Islands
which are my home, and have offered me so much.
I co-authored this book with a lot of aloha
and in hope of giving something back.

Contents

E komo mai!

E komo mai! Welcome.

This book will help you learn to weave with coconut leaves, called *lau niu* in Hawaiian. Also included are projects for people who already have weaving skills. The projects are arranged so that there is a progression of the basic styles of weaving one needs to know in order to complete the items.

Learning the techniques is relatively simple, but mastering the skills will take time and practice. After you have mastered the skills, your only limitation will be your imagination. Coconut weaving was a necessary skill in ancient Hawaiian times in order to create everyday household goods or items for ceremonial use. Today it can be considered an environmental art form, as it uses materials found in nature.

Along with the knowledge you obtain in this book comes the responsibility to take care of, *mālama,* the source of your natural materials, the tree. Since the focus of this book is weaving, we will not go into the maintenance and care of trees, but we will teach you how to select leaves without damaging this valuable resource.

Although the projects in this book can be done without any tools, some will be useful: a sharp knife, utility scissors, and a ball of string.

I dedicate this book to the Hawaiian Islands which are my home and have offered me so much. I co-authored it with a lot of aloha and in hopes of giving something back.

—Robert Morrison ("Haole Bob")

Introduction

In the earliest times, the *na kānaka maoli* (native human beings) were known to be practical survivalists and environmentalists. As the Polynesians ventured on voyages to find new lands and a new life, they learned to preserve and maximize available natural resources. Because of limited space to transport goods on the *wa'a* (canoe), the ancestors of ancient Hawaiians were careful in the selection of items to take on their voyages. Plants were selected for their many purposes. A valuable plant could serve as food, medicine, and construction material by making use of all its parts. The *kumu lau niu* (coconut tree), one of the most useful trees in existence, is an excellent example of maximizing a natural resource with minimum waste.

Some say that coconut palms originated in Malaya or Indonesia. Sanskrit records from before 1000 B.C. refer to the coconut palm in Asia, but Marco Polo wrote the first detailed European report of this unique tree, which he found in Sumatra in the thirteenth century. How coconut palms reached so many parts of the world is still a mystery. Coconut trees usually grow along the coastline, but they can survive at elevations up to three thousand feet. Some theorists suggest that the large, buoyant coconuts may have floated around the world on ocean currents, while others believe they were carried by man during explorations in the tropics.

Coconuts can grow in the wild, but most trees have been cultivated for thousands of years. The coconut is a vital and versatile plant to native peoples in the Caribbean islands, along the coast of Africa, and in South America, Malaya, India, Sri Lanka, Arab countries, the Philippines, and Polynesia. Because of its many uses, the coconut tree has been called the Tree of Life. It takes only a few trees to support a family. A few dozen trees could begin an exporting business.

The various uses of the coconut and tree seem to have been common knowledge among early native peoples around the world. The ingenuity and inventiveness of these different tropical cultures to independently maximize the value of the coconut is astonishing. As early as the eleventh century, Arab countries used coconut husks as a source for rope. Early voyagers made cordage and riggings from coconut fibers, and the dried fiber from the husks was also used to start fires. The coconut leaf was a valuable commodity too. It was used for construction of temporary housing—thatched roofs would last for an average of seven years—and for making household items such as brooms and baskets. Nutshells were made into containers.

The coconut itself is a single-seeded nut with a hard, woody shell encased in a thick, fibrous husk. Inside the hollow nut is a liquid known as coconut milk. Coconut milk obtained from young coconuts was commonly used in ancient times to treat numerous ailments, everything from washing open wounds to drinking for kidney problems. In addition to water, the milk contains sugars, enzymes, and vitamins, especially ascorbic acid (vitamin C). Other vitamins include folic acid, biotin, and riboflavin—all in the vitamin B complex—and pantothenic acid. The white kernel, or meat, of the coconut is also valuable as a staple food in the tropics, eaten raw or cooked.

The coconut tree is an important money crop. It is a source of timber, with trees growing to a height of 60 to 100 feet. Leaves are used to weave baskets and occasionally still today for thatch. Coconut oil, used for cooking and for body and hair ointments, is extracted from the dried white flesh of the coconut, called copra. Although the coconut is not commonly found in mainland supermarkets, it continues to be an important ingredient for many native cooks in the tropics. Food dishes include entrées of fish and seafood with coconut milk sauces to rich candies and desserts made with shredded coconut meat as well as with coconut milk.

Today refined coconut oil is used in high quality soaps, shampoos, shaving creams, and synthetic detergents because of its lathering properties. Drug, cosmetic, and chemical manufacturers continue to find new and improved products made from the oil as a base or additive. Still today, as it was thousands of years ago, the coconut is a valuable source for numerous items used in everyday life. See our next chapter for a couple of simple projects utilizing coconut trees.

References
Carolin Meyer. *Coconut: The Tree of Life.* Illustrated by Lynne Cherry. New York: William Morrow, 1976.

Lawrence K. Opeke. *Tropical Tree Corps.* New York: Wiley, 1982.

Lau Niu, Coconut Leaves

**The preparation and selection
of the *lau niu* fronds/leaves for weaving**

E ven though coconut trees are a hardy species that survive many natural conditions, they can be easily damaged by man. It is important to know that the young center leaves (or fronds) of the tree—usually from the first to the third or fourth budding frond—are vital to the tree's survival. If these leaves are cut the tree may die. There is a myth among some of today's weavers that you need to use very young leaves. That is not true. From my personal weaving experience, the number five to seven leaves out from the center are stronger and more durable than the first to fourth leaves. Taking these leaves will not damage the tree's main trunk *(kumu)*, the source of this natural material. Please keep in mind that it is not good practice to cut more that two fronds from a tree at one time. This enables the tree to remain balanced. For every leaf I take off, I wait a month before going back to that tree. This practice ensures the lasting source of natural weaving material.

My preference for a good leaf selection is that the leaf should be at least 39 inches in length, and the width should be an inch to an inch and a half, with an even taper. Also, the leaf should be spaced an inch apart from other leaves, with the rib of the leaf pliable enough to weave without breaking the rib.

Drying Process

Keep your supply of coconut leaves and projects made from them out of direct sunlight. Through experimentation, I have learned a few ways of drying coconut palm items.

If you want a light beige color, keep the item in a cool, dark place until it dries, usually for about a month. Freezing an item overnight will give it a dark color. Any time over twelve hours won't make it any darker. You can get a marble effect by lessening freezing time. Explore the possibilities.

When a coconut leaf project is just finished, you can microwave it for two minutes. This will bring the natural sap to the surface of the leaves. Set it on the counter, and note how soft and pliable it is. When the piece cools it will stiffen and have a beautiful satin glaze.

Tools

The projects in these chapters can be done without any tools, although some will be useful. These are: a simple, sharp knife, a utility scissors and a ball of string

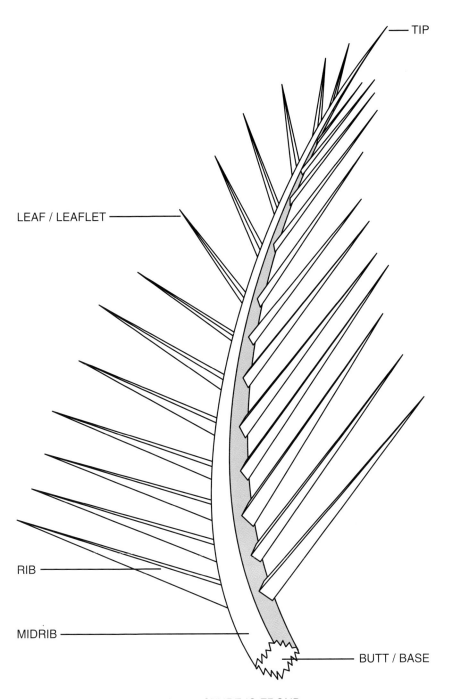

TIP

LEAF / LEAFLET

RIB

MIDRIB

BUTT / BASE

WHOLE PICTURE IS FROND

11

Chapter 1 *('Ekahi)*

Baskets for the Wall

Three basic projects are presented in this chapter: a heart basket, a wall basket, and a basic wall hanger. These were selected to provide you with the basic knowledge to progress from one weaving project to the next and on to the next chapter's projects.

Project 1
Heart Basket

Step 1:
Cut a section of frond with six leaves (at least 40 inches long) on each side of the frond. Then split the midrib down the middle.

13

Step 2:
Hold the two sections of the leaves together, as though they were on the frond. Then switch the positions R to L, L to R, with the rib facing up and the leaves facing in.

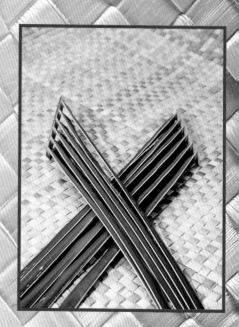

Step 3:
Hold the top leaves of each leaflet (at least) 8 inches from the midrib. Start plaiting across the top, left leaf over right leaf. Plait all of the leaves in that fashion.

Step 4:
Take the bottom two leaves (one will be facing left, the other right), then bend the left leaf over in the right direction to make a small loop. Cross the right leaf over the left leaf, and continue plaiting in that fashion for both sides.

Step 5:
All leaves should be pointing upward, six leaves to the left, and six leaves to the right. With the leaves pointing upward to the right, start with the leaf closest to the center, and bend and plait it toward the side of the basket. Once each sequential leaf reaches the side, plait it across the back six leaves toward the center. Plait the remaining leaves on the right side in the same fashion, working from the center leaves to the outside.

15

Step 6:
Repeat step 5 for the left side leaves, working from the center to the outside edge.

Step 7:
Turn the basket over with its back facing you. Now work with the ends of the leaves, starting with the end closest to the bottom. Lay the leaf over your index finger, and overlap the leaves in succession.

Hint: Working opposite sides, pull the leaves snugly as you go.

Step 8:
Tie the overlapping leaf ends into a knot, as close to the back as possible.

Step 9:
Turn the basket over and cut away leaf ends as close as possible to the midrib.

Hint: *Adjustment starts with the lowest leaf. Pull upward to secure an even shape.*

Final Step:
Trim the top leaves on either side into the semicircle, finishing on the top edge of the basket.

PAU!

Project 2
Wall Basket

Step 1:
Cut a section of frond with six leaves (at least 40 inches long) on each side of the frond.

Step 2:
Hold the two sections of the leaves together, as though they were on the frond. Then switch the positions R to L, L to R, with the rib facing up and the leaves facing in.

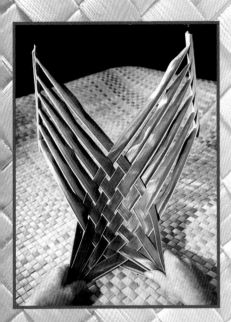

Step 3:
Hold the top leaves of each leaflet (at least) 8 inches from the midrib. Start plaiting across the top, left leaf over right leaf. Plait all of the leaves in that fashion.

Step 4:
Take the bottom two leaves (one will be facing left, the other right), then bend the left leaf over in the right direction to make a small loop. Cross the right leaf over the left leaf, and continue plaiting in that fashion for both sides.

19

Step 5:

All leaves should be pointing upward, six leaves to the left, and six leaves to the right. Start with the leaves pointing upward to the right. Take an outside leaf and plait it across the back of the six leaves, upward toward the cneter. Plait the remaining leaves in sequence. Repeat for the left side.

Hint: Cross behind the first two leaves to have the plaiting process come out correctly.

Step 6:

Starting with the centermost three leaves, make a French braid. Each time you make a fold to the braid, the next leaf will be added. Fold and add successive leaves sequentially from either side into the center braid.

Hint: As the leaves are incorporated into the braid, the leaf sections get wider and wider, so expand the back until all the leaves have been added.

Final Step:

Continue with the French braid, leaving 3 inches to tie a knot for closure. The wall basket is now finished unless it needs to be trimmed and shaped.

PAU!

 Bonus Project: *Lau Niu* **Rake**

After a cluster of coconuts has been cut from a tree, the part holding the coconut blossom can make a handy rake. Carefully remove coconuts from the blossom, and your rake is ready to use.

Project 3
Basic Wall Hanger

Step 1:
Select a section of frond with a leaflet at least 39 inches long. Cut a section of frond with six leaves on each side, leaving both sides attached.

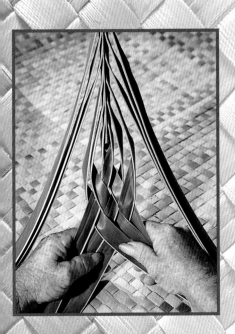

Step 2:
Plait all leaves, working with the bottom leaves upward.

Hint: Six leaves should be pointing or leaning left and six pointing right.

Step 3:
Work with the leaves pointing to the right. Starting with the #2 leaf, bend it behind the #3 leaf, plaiting upward toward the #6 leaf. Now finish plaiting the #2 leaf across the back toward the center. Plait the #1 leaf (without bending it), starting at the #3 leaf toward the #6 leaf, then across the back toward the center. Plait the #1 leaf into leaves 3, 4, 5, and 6, as you did #2. Leave the ends of the leaves sticking out the back.

Hint: The numbering of leaves starts with #1 being the bottom leaf.

Step 4:
Repeat step 3 for the left side.

23

Step 5:
Turn the basket over, and bring all the leaves together, pointing straight up. Cut about 6 inches up from the back of the basket.

Step 6:
Work with both sides, starting with the bottom leaf, right side plaited toward the left, over the midrib. Then leaves on the left side are plaited toward the right, over the midrib.

Hint: *The plaiting process isn't only for looks. This is a locking process, and the best result is achieved by going under two leaves. (See photo.)*

Final Step:
Cut all loose ends.

PAU!

 Bonus Project: *Lau Niu* **Broom**

You'll need about 80 leaflets to make a nice broom. The leaflets don't have to be fresh or young (actually, older leaflets work better than fresh ones). Strip the ribs away from the leaves–a knife or thumbnail works well. Then gather together all the ribs with the thick part at one end and make a bundle. Tie the bundle very tightly with cord or whatever string you have on hand. Usually tying in two places about four inches apart works well. Then cut the smaller ends flush. Pau–you have made a great hand broom.

Chapter 2 *('Elua)*

Other Hanging Projects

We begin here with two variations of the basic wall hanger (project 3): the fancy wall hanger and the double wall hanger. Project 6, the plant hanging basket, is a different style, which will allow you to progress to Chapter 3.

Project 4
Fancy Wall Hanger

Note: The fancy wall hanger weave is the same as the basic wall hanger you learned in chapter 1, with a couple of extra leaves for frills.

Step 1:
Cut a section of frond with 16 leaves (at least 39 inches long) on each side, leaving both sides attached.

Step 2:

Weave like the basic wall hanger, using only six leaves. Start with the ninth leaf from the top. The top three leaves will be used for frill.

Step 3:

Pull together three leaves from the R side, with the first three leaves under the basket not woven. Pull together the tips, and bring them upward around the back side of the top three leaves not woven. From the back side of the basket, take the three leaves and push them through the midrib to the front. The tips will be facing you. Then insert those leaves from front to back on the other side, crossing the midrib.

Step 4:

Repeat step 3 for the L side.

Step 5:
With six leaves pointing out the back, tie a double knot and cut the excess leaf endings, leaving one inch past the knot.

Step 6:
Turn the basket over facing you. Starting with the very bottom leaf on either side, cut off at the midrib (work with the R side first). On the next leaf up, cut a quarter inch in from the previous leaf edge. Keep cutting in sequence.

OTHER HANGING PROJECTS

Final Step:
Work the other side as in
step 6, and cut to match.

PAU!

Bonus Project: Barbecue Grill Cleaner

After husking a coconut, save the husk. Let it dry for
about a week. With the fibers down, rub the husk
across the barbecue grill until it is clean.

30

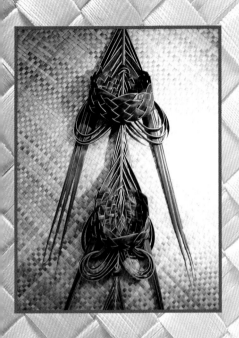

Project 5
Double Wall Hanger

Note: *The double wall hanger is basically made the same as the fancy wall hanger (project 4), except that you will need to start out with a section of at least 27 leaves.*

Step 1:
Cut a section of frond with (at least) 27 leaves on each side, leaving both sides attached.

Note: *Steps 2–5 are the same as for the fancy wall hanger (project 4).*

Step 2:
Weave like the basic wall hanger (project 3), using only six leaves. Start with the ninth leaf from the top. The top three leaves will be used for frill.

31

Step 3:

Pull together three leaves from the R side, with the first three leaves under the basket not woven. Pull together the tips, and bring them upward around the back side of the top three leaves not woven. From the back side of the basket, take the three leaves and push them through the midrib to the front. The tips will be facing you. Then insert those leaves from front to back on the other side, crossing the midrib.

Step 4:

Repeat step 3 for the L side.

Step 5:

With six leaves pointing out the back, tie a double knot and cut the excess leaf endings, leaving one inch past the knot.

Step 6:

Repeat steps 2–5 for the second basket. Start with the first leaf underneath the finished basket.

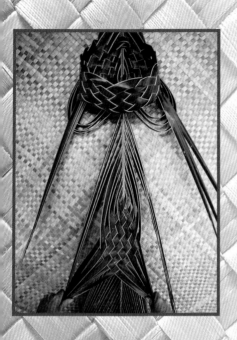

Step 7:
Turn the basket over facing you. Starting with the very bottom leaf on either side, cut off at the midrib (work with R side first). At the next leaf up, cut a quarter inch in from the previous leaf edge. Keep cutting in sequence.

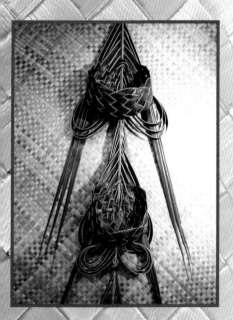

Final Step:
Work the other side, and cut to match.

PAU!

Project 6
Plant Hanging Basket

Step 1:
Select a section on the one side of a frond with 16 leaves that are the same width and at least 40 inches long. Take a leaf off each end, and shave the midrib thin enough to make an even circle when it's bent.

Step 2:
Hold the leaves in one hand with the midrib facing down.

Step 3:
Cut where the first leaf was pulled off, so that the leaves will be evenly spaced when a circle is tied.

Step 4:
Making a circle, cut two notches on the midrib, and let the circle go. Hold the leaf with the midrib facing you, and cut two more notches on the opposite side, even with the first cut. Repeat the same cuts on the other end.

Step 5:

Bend the frond into a circle, lining up the notches. Tie the circle with string, leaving plenty of string at each end. Wrap one end of the string around the midrib and notches, going in one direction. Then wrap the other end of the string around the midrib and the other notches, in the opposite direction. Tie three knots and cut off the excess string.

Step 6:

Hold the circle in your left hand, with the leaf rib facing up. Start with any leaf, and fold it over the leaf in front. Continue using the rest of the leaves, locking the last leaf through the first leaf and folding to complete the circle.

Step 7:

Turn upside down and gather all leaves, holding them upward. Take out one leaf. Starting with the one in the front, count seven leaves in the direction they are leaning. With the leaf hanging out, bring it across the leaves to the opposite side of the circle and insert it under the seventh leaf.

Step 8:

Start with the first leaf behind the leaf you just inserted, and bring it across the circle through the sixth leaf. In that fashion finish the circle.

Step 9:

Start with any leaf and plait one time in the direction it's leaning or pointing. Continue plaiting the rest of the leaves in the same fashion. Pull in all the leaf ends to even up the basket shape.

Note: You are pulling tight enough only to even up the basket, not to lock the weave.

Step 10:

Plait all leaf ends one more time. Now start with any leaf end and pull to tighten. The second leaf you will be working with is the leaf overlapping at the bottom of the basket.

Note: You are pulling to tighten and shape the bottom.

Step 11:

To make the handles, use six leaves for each side. The leaves should be pointing or leaning in one direction. Starting with any two leaves, the first leaf will be crossed in the front of the second leaf. The third leaf will be added behind the second leaf. Now add the fourth leaf, plaiting it across the others. Finish plaiting the fifth and sixth leaves.

Step 12:

Take the bottom leaf, and bend and plait it back across the handle. Bend the bottom leaf on the opposite side and plait it across the handle. Working from the opposite sides, finish plaiting toward the end of the leaves. Leave enough ends to tie a knot using all the leaves. Tie a knot.

Step 13:

There will be eight leaves left. Using the center six leaves, make the other handle (the same as in step 12).

Note: When plaiting toward the end of the second handle, pull the handles together and plait until they are even.

Step 14:

Using the two extra leaves, bend and plait them into the basket and pull tightly.

Final Step:
Cut off the excess leaf ends.
Tie the tops of the handles
together with string just
below the knots.

PAU!

 Bonus Project: Hanging Planter

The coconut husk makes a great hanging pot. Take care
when husking a coconut to keep the bottom attached.
After the nut is removed, trim the top with a knife so
there will be room for a plant. Bind it with cord or a
small rope and hang. The husk retains moisture for the
plant. These last for years.

Chapter 3 (*'Ekolu*)

Fancy Baskets

The three projects in this chapter are a fruit basket, a trash basket, and a flower vase. They are all more complex in design than the previous projects. Before heading into this chapter, you should feel comfortable working the projects in chapters 1 and 2.

Project 7
Fruit Basket

Step 1:
Select a section on the one side of the frond with 16 leaves that are the same width and at least 40 inches long. Take a leaf off each end, and shave the midrib thin enough to make an even circle when it's bent.

Step 2:
Hold the leaves in one hand, with the midrib facing down.

Step 3:
Cut where the first leaf was pulled off, so that leaves will be spaced evenly when a circle is tied.

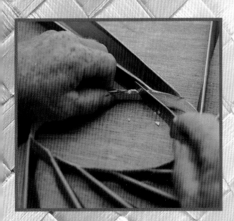

Step 4:
Making a circle, cut two notches on the midrib, and let the circle go. Hold the leaf with the midrib facing you, and cut two more notches on the opposite side, even with the first cut. Repeat the same cuts on the other end.

Step 5:

Bend the frond into a circle, lining up the notches. Tie the circle with string, leaving plenty of string at each end. Wrap one end of the string around the midrib and notches, going in one direction. Then wrap the other end of the string around the midrib and the other notches, in the opposite direction. Tie three knots and cut off the excess string.

Step 6:

Hold the circle with the leaflets rib facing down. You will be working in the direction the leaves are pointing. Starting with any leaf, weave under the first leaf, then over and under the next six leaves. Continue working in the direction the leaves are pointing, finishing the rest of the leaves around the circle.

FANCY BASKETS

Step 7:
Turn the bowl upside down, with the leaves going down. To tighten and even the basket, start with any leaf and pull it tightly at the midrib. Continue to pull each leaf down snug. This process should be repeated until the weaving is evenly tightened.

Step 8:
Turn the bowl right side up. Looking through the center of the bowl, push all the leaves through the bottom.

Step 9:

Start by turning the bowl upside down and holding all leaves upward. Take out one leaf, starting with the leaf in front, and count seven leaves in the direction they are leaning. Start with the leaf hanging out and bring it across the leaves on the opposite side of the circle, inserting it under the seventh leaf.

Step 10:

Start with the first leaf behind the leaf you just inserted, and bring it across the circle through the sixth leaf.

Step 11:

In that fashion, finish the bottom circle. Grasp one leaf and the opposite side leaf, then pull away from the bowl. Keep going with the same process, working in the direction that the leaves overlap at the center of the bowl.

Note: Pull leaves just snug, but not too tight.

Step 12:

This step adjusts the star pattern at the bottom of the bowl. Star leaves tend to bend in the opposite direction than they should be going. Turn the bowl upright. Working from the inside and outside, hold a finger at the intersection of leaves and push upward on the star leaf from the bottom. Turn the bowl over. Working as before, pull on the opposite leaves to tighten a little at a time. Finish tightening until the bottom is flat with the circle.

Note: While tightening the bottom, check the star from inside; some leaves may need readjustment.

Final Step:

Optional: cut the tips of the leaves. To finish the bowl, weave the ends of the leaves and plait them outside the bowl. Cut off excess leaf ends

PAU!

Project 8
Trash Basket

Step 1:
Select a section with a total of 20 leaves on both sides of a frond that are the same width and at least 40 inches long. Then split the frond in half at the midrib. Take a leaf off each end, and shave the midrib thin enough to make an even circle when it's bent.

Step 2:
Hold the leaves in one hand, with the midrib facing down.

Step 3:

Cut where the first leaf was pulled off, so that the leaves will be spaced evenly when a circle is tied.

Step 4:

Making a circle, cut two notches on the midrib, and let the circle go. Hold the leaf with the midrib facing you, and cut two more notches on the opposite side, even with the first cut. Repeat the same cuts on the other end.

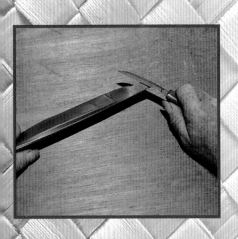

Step 5:
Bend the frond into a circle, lining up the notches. Tie the circle with string, leaving plenty of string at either end. Wrap one end of the string around the midrib and notches, going in one direction. Then wrap the other end of the string around the midrib and the other notches, in the opposite direction. Tie three knots and cut off the excess string.

Step 6:
Hold the circle in your left hand, with the leaf rib facing up. Start with any leaf and fold it over the leaf in front. Continue using the rest of the leaves, locking the last leaf through the first leaf and folding to complete the circle.

Step 7:
Make a circle with the other side of the frond, repeating steps 1–6.

Note: *The leaves will be facing in the opposite direction.*

FANCY BASKETS

Step 8:
Hold the circles in each hand about shoulder length apart, with the leaves facing each other, away from you..

Step 9:
Cross one leaf from each circle. Start the plaiting process by adding one leaf from each side. Continue adding leaves, plaiting with only six leaves at a time. Finish going around the circle, interlocking with leaves already plaited.

Step 10:
Then interlock and plait one end all the way out to the edge of the circle. Leaves should be facing outward, away from the basket. Repeat this step for the opposite side.

Step 11:
At one end, start pulling and snuggling up the leaves, evening up the side walls of the trash basket.

Step 12:
Working with the side that will be the top, start with any leaf. Fold the leaf downward and plait it back into the sides.

Step 13:

At the other end (the bottom), plait the leaves through to the inside.

Step 14:

Hold all leaves together and cut leaf tips. Pull out one leaf, count ten, and with the one pulled out leaf cross over the leaves to the opposite side of the circle and insert it through the tenth leaf. Then lock the leaf into the folded leaf on the outside of the circle. Continue with sequential leaves. Then pull tight with the opposite side leaves, two at a time.

Note: There should be a star design on the bottom.

Final Step:
Plait leaf ends down the outside, and even up the top and bottom to straighten the trash can. Cut excess leaf tips.

PAU!

Project 9
Flower Vase

Step 1:
Select a section on the one side of a frond with 14 leaves that are the same width and at least 39 inches long. Take a leaf off each end, and shave the midrib thin enough to make an even circle when it's bent.

Step 2:
Cut where the first leaf was pulled off, so that the leaves will be evenly spaced where the circle is tied.

Step 3:
Make a circle and cut two notches on the midrib.

Step 4:
Holding the leaf with the midrib facing you, cut two more notches on the opposite sides, even with the first cut. Repeat the same cuts at the other end.

Step 5:

Bend the frond into a circle, lining up the notches. Tie the circle with string, leaving plenty of string at each end. Wrap one end of the string around the midrib and notches, going in one direction. Then wrap the other end of the string around the midrib and the other notches, in the opposite direction. Tie three knots and cut off the excess string.

Step 6:

Repeat steps 1–5 with the other side of the frond.

Note: One circle might be a little larger than the other. If so, use the smaller circle for step 7. The larger circle will not be folded the same as the smaller circle.

Step 7:

Hold the circle in your left hand, with the leaf rib facing up. Start with any leaf and fold it over the leaf in front. Continue using the rest of the leaves, locking the last leaf through the first leaf and folding to complete the circle.

Step 8:
Place the larger circle underneath the smaller circle, with leaf ribs upward. Take any leaf and start plaiting, adding leaves sequentially around the bottom circle. Holding the leaves in your left hand, keep adding leaves until the desired height is attained.

Step 9:
After the desired height is attained, begin the locking process. The leaves will be pointing or leaning in two directions. Select the direction in which the leaves are the shortest. Then lock these by folding each leaf downward, plaiting down the outside of the vase.

Step 10:

This is the tightening process. Stand the vase upside down. Start with any locked leaf, and hold its tip between your thumb and index finger. Place your thumb underneath the bend of that leaf, pushing with an upward motion. Pull any slack downward from the tip of the leaf. You will need to go around a few times to evenly shape the vase. This is a slow process.

Step 11:

Lay the vase on its side. Slightly push down and pull on unlocked leaves, one at a time, to shape the bottom. Continue tightening the unlocked leaves.

Step 12:
Repeat the process with the locked and unlocked leaves until the desired shape and tightness are achieved. Tighten so that the vase is level when standing up. Finish plaiting the loose ends of the locked leaves; plaiting three to four times will be sufficient. Do not cut loose ends off yet.

Step 13:
For the bottom, hold all leaves up, bring one leaf out, and count seven leaves. Take the one leaf that is out and insert it under the sixth leaf. Continue with the leaf behind the one just used, bringing it across and inserting it behind the fifth leaf. Continue weaving leaves in this fashion.

Step 14:
Gradually start pulling any leaf to tighten snugly. Move on to the next leaf and do the same.

Step 15:
Hold all leaf ends together and cut off leaf ends.

Step 16:
Finish off the bottom by plaiting the remaining loose leaves up the side. If you have enough leaf length, plait three to four times.

Final Step:
Tighten all bottom leaves and cut loose ends. Then tighten the remaining leaves and cut loose ends.

PAU KA PUKE!

Glossary

Hawaiian words and phrases

'ekahi	one, first
'ekolu	three, third
'elua	two, second
kumu	tree trunk; source
lau	leaf or leaves
lau niu	coconut leaf or frond
mālama	take care of, preserve
niu	coconut palm
pau	finished
pau ka puke	the book (is) finished

English words and phrases

adjustment	process of tightening and pulling leaves to shape basket
bend	twisting leaf so rib will go from top to bottom or bottom to top
circle	bringing both ends of a section together and tying at notches with string
cross	beginning of plaiting process
french braid	braiding with three leaves
fold	bending leaf to lock it under leaf in front of it

frond	combination of all the midrib leaf and rib
interlock	to plait
L	left; left side
leaf/leaflet	a single leaf section, protruding from either side of midrib
leaf ends	tips of the leaf or leaves, remaining after weaving
lock	plaiting ends of leaves into crossing leaves
loose ends	leftover leaf tips
midrib	center structure of frond holding leaves
notches	evenly cut triangles spaced 1/8 inch apart at ends of midrib
plait/plaiting	weaving process of over and under, interlocking the leaves
R	right; right side
rib	thin hard center or backbone of leaves
section	a number of leaves cut from a frond, still joined at midrib
sequentially	use of each leaf in its order
star	center design at bottom of basket
tightening	process of pulling leaves to strengthen and shape basket

Acknowledgments

I especially thank Electra-Eyed Photography, Randy Morrison (my brother), for coming to Hawai'i to do the beautiful interior photography for this book.

I want to thank the many weavers from Tahiti, Bora Bora, Palau, Samoa, and the Hawaiian Islands who shared their styles and techniques with me. Special thanks go to Uncle Harry from 'Ewa, who had the patience to teach me in the beginning.

Also a big mahalo to you, Auntie Healani. I've learned a lot from you while working on this project about your love for the Hawaiian culture. I never would have done it without you.

Even though I weave in my own style, I appreciate and value the traditional arts of weaving with *lau niu.*